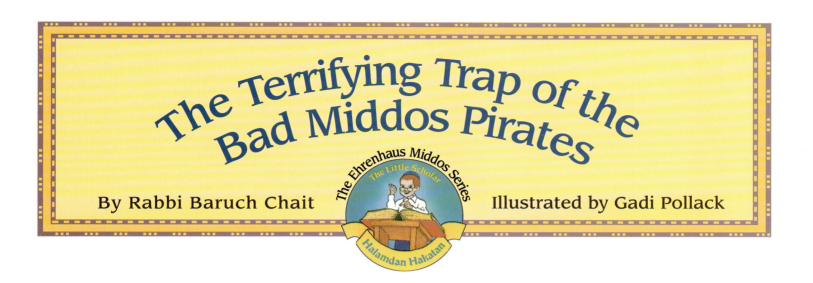

MIDDOS SERIES 3

———

THE LOBOS EDITION

Graphic Design: Ben Gasner

To Our Darling
JESSICA AND MELISSA,
FROM YOUR LOVING PARENTS

Our Sages teach us:
"אם אין דרך ארץ, אין תורה" פרקי אבות ג כא

May you always treat others with respect
and may your lives be guided
by the principles found in this book.

In Honor of Our Dear Children,
TOVY, MOSHE MEIR, and **SHMULY**

May we continue to derive
much joy and satisfaction from you
in the many years to come.
May you continue
to personify the character traits
that are portrayed in this book.

ARI & YONA BERGMANN

To Our Parents

RUTH & KALMEN SILBER

VERONICA KOLTAI MORDECHAI Hacohen FRIEDMANN ע״ה

To Our Children

EDA & DANI   **ESTHER & BEREL**   **COOKIE**

And to Our Grandchildren

**ELIYAHU   NECHAMA HINDA   EMUNAH
MORDECHAI YAAKOV   ILANA   ALIZA**

Dedicated by
EVA & CHAIM SILBER

Dedicated in Memory of Our Dear Parents

הר״ה נתן ב״ר מאיר לימן ז״ל
נלב״ע כ״ז תמוז תשנ״ה

מרת בתיה בת הר״ר יונה לימן ע״ה
נלב״ע כ״ה תשרי תשנ״ו

Who, by example, taught us how to build character
and focused, in particular, on עין טובה and לב טוב

THE LEHMAN FAMILY

To Our Dear Children and Grandchildren

May you always try to develop
your good middos and lev tov

צאו וראו איזוהי דרך ישרה שידבק בה האדם.
רבי אלעזר אומר: לב טוב.

CHANTAL & MARC
NAHVA, MICHAL, TALIA, YONI, PINCHUS, BORUCH ELISHA

NAOMI & ALAIN
BELLA, DANIELLA, YAEL, HADASSAH, AVIGAYIL

ROCHIE & LAURENT
SIMI, CHASI, AKIVA

SAMMY, LIORA & DAVID, MOISHELE

with love,
VERA & SOLI SPIRA

DEDICATED TO THE MEMORY OF THE MELTZ FAMILY
Woodstock, New Brunswick, Canada
FROM THE ALLIE C. MELTZ ESTATE

אליהו חנא בן נתן הכהן י"ב סיון תשנ"ב

NATHAN
אביו נתן בר' חיים הכהן ג' תמוז תשי"א

RACHEL
אמו רחל לאה בת ר' אליהו י"ב שבט תרצ"ו

REBECCA
אחותו ראשע רבקה בת ר' נתן הכהן י"ד שבט תש"ל

DORA
אחותו חאשע דבורה בת ר' נתן הכהן ח' שבט תשט"ז

SAMUEL
אחיו זלמן שמחה בר' נתן הכהן כ"ז טבת תשל"ג

JAMES
אחיו שמואל יוסף בר' נתן הכהן כ"ו תמוז תשכ"א

HASKAMAH

It is with great pleasure that I write this letter of *Haskamah* for the wonderful new book on middos written by Rav Baruch Chait שליט"א. This book is an unusual combination of scholarship, creativity and artistry, which compliments and beautifies the sacred teachings of our holy Torah. His first book, *The 39 Avoth Melacha of Shabbath*, was a huge success and was indeed a tremendous contribution to the Jewish community. It effectively enhanced an appreciation and understanding of the laws and the significance of the Shabbath to students on every level and almost every age.

The *Incredible Voyage to Good Middos* and *The Lost Treasure of Tikun HaMiddos Island* are books which take the very important and difficult task of teaching middos, and make it an enjoyable and challenging experience rather than an insurmountable burden. These books, which are based on the sefer *Orchos Tzaddikim*, are woven around the story of a well-known historical event with some interesting original revisions. They embellish the basic Torah hashkafah with an intriguing plot and subtle allegorical messages. They combine many significant mussar principles with very important fundamental ethical guidelines.

Even amongst the most religious Torah communities today there is a great need for the emphasis and development of a proper middos-training program for children and adults. Improvement in the areas of mutual respect, love and compassion are sorely needed to offset deeply rooted negative feelings of bitterness, animosity and hatred toward other Jews. Good middos are the basis of our entire Torah; אם אין דרך ארץ אין תורה and is the essence of all Jewish values. Minimum levels of ואהבת לרעך כמוך and a meaningful level of true יראת שמים cannot be reached without good middos. Only through working and developing our character can we possibly rectify the שנאת חינם which was the cause of the destruction of our Holy Temple and only then will we be זוכה to bring the *Mashiach*.

May הקב"ה bless Harav Baruch Chait שליט"א with much הצלחה in this "incredible" project. May he be זוכה with his family to many years of good health and may he continue his great work in הרבצת התורה.

Rabbi Chaim P. Scheinberg

הרב חיים פנחס שיינברג
ראש ישיבת "תורה אור"
ומורה הוראה דקרית מטרסדורף

Rabbi Chaim P. Scheinberg
Kiryat Mattersdorf
Jerusalem, Israel

ACKNOWLEDGMENTS

All those who have greatly assisted me with the publication of volume one *The Incredible Voyage to Good Middos* and volume two *The Lost Treasure of Tikun HaMiddos Island*, have assisted me with this third volume *The Terrifying Trap of the Bad Middos Pirates*, and I would like to express my appreciation to them.

My dear parents: Rabbi & Mrs. Moshe Chait *Shlita*
My dear wife and children: Paula Chait and Family
My devoted Rosh Yeshiva: Harav Henach Leibowitz *shlita*

A special thanks to my dearest friends
Chaim and Eva Silber and Family
for always being part of all my projects

My deepest appreciation to
Nancy and Shimmy Katz and Family
founders of "Halamdan Hakatan" Series for their continuous support

Our dedicated staff and associates:
Gadi Pollack: *artist*
Mrs. Sheryl Prenzlau: *editorial advisor*
Mrs. Devorah Rhein: *editor*
Reb Chaim BenMoshe: *source material*
Rabbi Dovid Chait: *advisory board*
Mrs. Naomi Chait: *editorial advisory board*
Ben Gasner: *graphics director*
Nili Boim, Leah Green: *graphics*

I also want to thank the staff and students of Ma'arava Machon Rubin and our dear friends who have helped us with our previous publications.

Rabbi Ari and Yona Bergmann
Jack and Doris Bistricer
Prof. Jacob and Rachel Dolinger
Jack and Faigi Ehrenhaus
Isaac and Edie Gross
Dr. Dov and Marlene Heller
Murray and Laura Huberfeld
Patrick and Caroline Landau
Melech and Elaine Lehman
Jay and Huti Pomrenze
Dr. Lindsay and Rivki Rosenwald
Moshe and Elaine Rubin
Mrs. Rose Scharf
Marty and Melodie Scharf
Richard and Dana Scharf
Barry and Bonnie Septimus
Soli and Vera Spira
Ushi and Esti Stahler
Larry Traub
Arie and Chaney Wolfson
Reb P & Reb A

INTRODUCTION

Parts 1 and 2 of the *middos series* deal with the middah of *gaavah* as explained in the *Orchos Tzaddikim*. Parts 3 and 4 and are based on the next ten middos brought in that *sefer,* following *gaavah and anavah.* Most of the ideas in this book are based on the *Orchos Tzaddikim,* unless otherwise indicated.

OUTLINE OF STORY

1. The *Anavah* boat is lured off course, attacked and captured. The travelers are then brought to the Fortress of the Bad Middos Pirates.

2. The travelers are tried in Pirate Court and found guilty and punished. They are separated into small groups and placed into the ten chambers of the Bad Middos Pirates in an attempt to destroy the travelers' good middos. The travelers stand firm with courage. They rebuke the Pirates and criticize their behavior, hoping to have a good influence on them. The travelers are unsuccessful and the Pirates' bad behavior influences the travelers instead.

In this section the words of the travelers appear in bold italic type. In various places on each page, there are small Pirates who appear in white balloons that illustrate the type of corrected behavior the travelers were hoping to see as a result of their remarks. In each case, their efforts were unsuccessful.

3. The travelers attempt to escape from the Fortress but can't. They begin to despair...
4. Suddenly, Rebbe Lev Tov's boat appears in the distance and the travelers are certain that he has come to save them. When the Chief Pirate arrives on that boat, the travelers are shocked.
5. Rebbe Lev Tov reveals his past and inspires all the Bad Middos Pirates to change their ways.
6. The Fortress is turned into a beautiful Palace where people come from all over the world to learn good middos.

The subject of Middos is a very difficult one to teach effectively. We hope this somewhat unusual approach will be enjoyed, well received, and effectual.

Hi! I'm Yankele and I'm back to tell you all about the next exciting episode of our story.

As I'm sure you remember, in the first book, *The Incredible Voyage to Good Middos*, Rebbe Lev Tov met the travelers who were sailing on the ship, the *Gaavatanic,* and were leaving Eretz Yisrael to find the excitement of Glitterland.

Rebbe Lev Tov tried to warn them that they must improve their middos or they would be headed for disaster, but the travelers wouldn't listen. When the *Gaavatanic* hit an iceberg and started sinking, Rebbe Lev Tov was there to rescue them, and he brought them safely to the island of Tikun Hamiddos.

In the second book, *The Lost Treasure of Tikun Hamiddos Island,* the travelers were taught many lessons on the island about good middos. When their middos were greatly improved, they were ready to go back home to Eretz Yisrael. However, they had no way to travel because their boat, the *Gaavatanic,* had sunk. With Rebbe Lev Tov's guidance, the travelers worked together very hard and built the *Anavah* boat from the debris of the *Gaavatanic.*

Although the *Anavah* was small and looked very fragile, it was really quite stable, and the tired travelers sailed along happily on their way back home to Eretz Yisrael.

And now we follow the weary *Anavah* travelers as they approach the final stretch of their dangerous journey…

The *Anavah* was sailing on the high seas, heading as fast as it could go toward its final destination, Eretz Yisrael. The ocean can be very dangerous at times, but so far the boat and its passengers were safely on course and making good time. If everything went as scheduled, they would be home in just a few more days.

To some of the passengers, Eretz Yisrael still seemed to be very far away and they felt that they would never get there. This made them irritable and impatient and they began complaining about everything, especially their poor living conditions and the lack of good food. "Don't you remember our beautiful ship, the *Gaavatanic*, and the luxurious life we once had?" one of the travelers asked. They conveniently forgot about all the troubles their bad middos had caused them. Some started thinking again about the Glitterland they had once looked for. "Maybe now is the time to try to find the Glitterland we never found!" someone shouted. "How much longer can we possibly wait to get to Eretz Yisrael?"

The *yetzer hara* always looks for the opportunity to pounce on people when they are weak and vulnerable. And so, the very moment the passengers began to complain and think about changing their route, the *yetzer hara* moved into position and was ready to attack and take complete control.

In the distance, hidden behind a thick patch of fog, a huge, dangerous pirate ship was quietly making its way along the waters, searching for its next prey. On the bow of the ship stood "Jealous Jake," the ferocious pirate, who was peering through his telescope, just waiting to find something new to be jealous of. He almost missed the small and simple *Anavah* boat, but the irritating sound of loud voices complaining and yelling caught his attention. Jealous Jake turned his telescope toward the noise and spotted what seemed to be a poor, small, harmless-looking boat. But then he thought to himself, "Although this small, flimsy boat doesn't seem so valuable, the fact that it is traveling so far out in the middle of the ocean must mean that it is on an important mission, and it is probably carrying some very important cargo. I bet those travelers are hiding great treasures of silver and gold and are using this small, innocent looking boat as a disguise, so that no one will suspect it."

Jealous Jake was sure that besides the valuables, the boat would have many cannons and weapons on board for protection, so he tried to think of a good plan to capture the boat and steal all the treasures. "Aha! I have it!" he cried. "Why not use the power of my good old reliable buddy, the *Yetzer Hara,* to tempt them! Once they fall for the temptations, they will be within my grasp, and very, very easy to catch."

As the *Anavah* continued sailing along the ocean waters, unaware of the dangers lurking nearby, the passengers saw what appeared to be a very large, strange sign floating in the distance.

The sign said, "Stop now for a delicious Glatt Kosher Surprise with 'fries' and "Try Jake's Juicy *Tayvah* Burger." They just had to turn left and 'sink' their teeth into the scrumptious, mouth-watering delights.

The weary travelers, who had been living on simple, practically tasteless food since their ship, the *Gaavatanic*, went down, were very tempted by the picture of that scrumptious burger. "It can't hurt to go just a little bit off course to get such a wonderful meal," someone said. "This might even give us more strength to carry on for the rest of our journey," others declared. "This is a gift from heaven!" "We can surely use a break from all this traveling. Let's go!"

The captain was very concerned. He didn't think it was safe to go off course, because they might lose their way and never find the right direction again. He pleaded with the other passengers, saying that it just wasn't worth taking the chance. He even reminded them of how Rebbe Lev Tov always used to tell them, "One little wrong turn can take you very, very far from your destination." He was also very suspicious about who would be selling Glatt Kosher Burgers way out in the middle of the ocean.

But the travelers were too excited to listen to him after having seen that picture of the delicious burger sandwich and dreaming of all the other wonderful goodies they were sure they would find at Jake's. All they could think about was how hungry they were, and how they wanted to get something good and tasty to eat *right now*. They were no longer able to hear the advice of those who knew better than they did!

And so, despite the captain's misgivings, the little boat turned left at the sign, and headed for Jake's Juicy *Tayvah* Burger, where the delicious lunch they imagined would be waiting for them. Little did they know just how much this decision that was guided purely by temptation would cost them. The "Glatt Kosher Surprise with Fries" turned out to be a much bigger surprise than they could ever have imagined -- and *they* were almost the Fries!

There wasn't really a burger restaurant way out there in the middle of the ocean at all! The sign was actually the trap that Jealous Jake had set for them. He planned to take the *Anavah* travelers back to the island where he and his friends, the Bad Middos Pirates, would steal all their treasures and take "good" care of them.

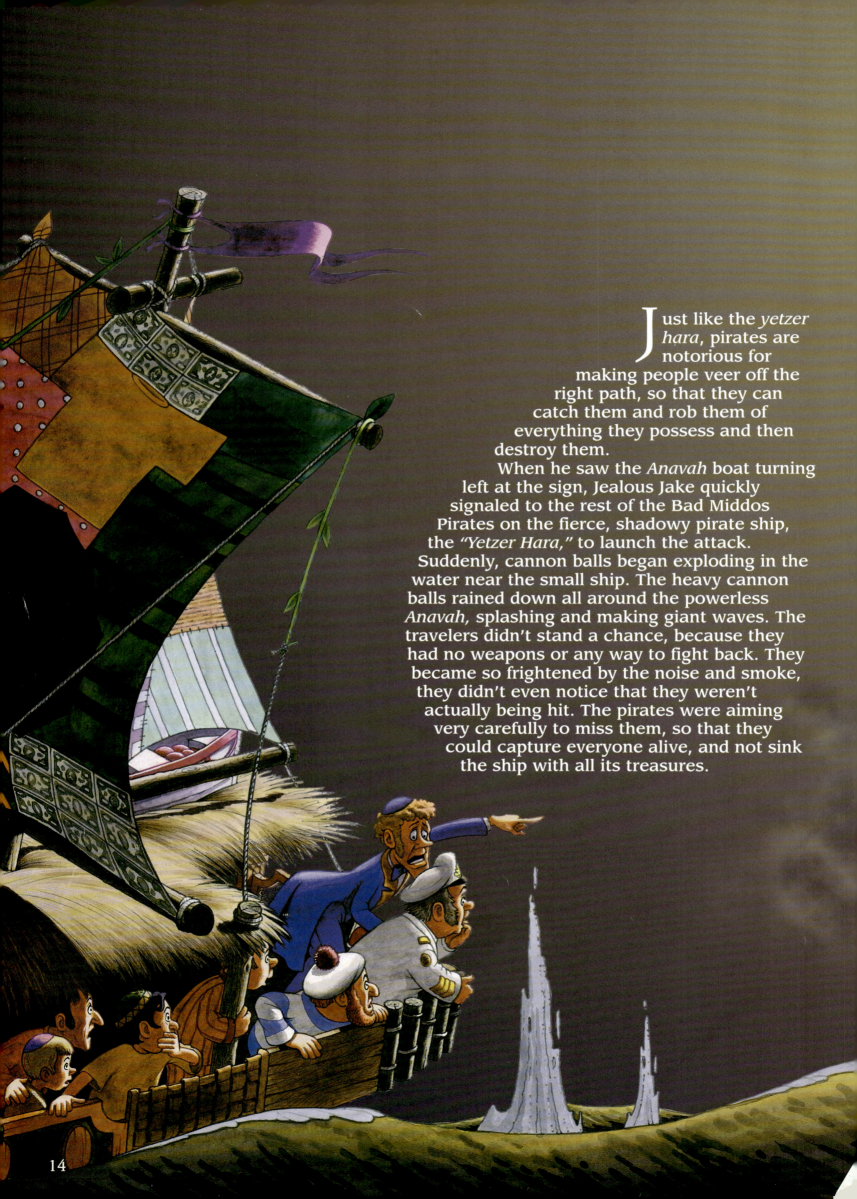

Just like the *yetzer hara*, pirates are notorious for making people veer off the right path, so that they can catch them and rob them of everything they possess and then destroy them.

When he saw the *Anavah* boat turning left at the sign, Jealous Jake quickly signaled to the rest of the Bad Middos Pirates on the fierce, shadowy pirate ship, the *"Yetzer Hara,"* to launch the attack. Suddenly, cannon balls began exploding in the water near the small ship. The heavy cannon balls rained down all around the powerless *Anavah*, splashing and making giant waves. The travelers didn't stand a chance, because they had no weapons or any way to fight back. They became so frightened by the noise and smoke, they didn't even notice that they weren't actually being hit. The pirates were aiming very carefully to miss them, so that they could capture everyone alive, and not sink the ship with all its treasures.

As the pirate ship came closer, the people on the *Anavah* looked up and saw a dark cloud suspended directly over their heads. The cloud seemed to float in the air for a few seconds before falling down right on top of their ship! As they twisted helplessly within the cloud, the travelers gradually realized that it wasn't really a cloud at all, but a huge, dark net that the pirates had shot from their main cannon. The net covered the entire boat and all the passengers were trapped under it.

When the Bad Middos Pirates were sure that the passengers on the *Anavah* were incapable of getting away, they pulled the little *Anavah* boat along with them. Later, they scrambled aboard and searched it thoroughly from top to bottom for the silver and gold they thought was hidden there. They looked in every nook and cranny, but they couldn't find a thing. This made the pirates furious and they threatened to punish the passengers in the worst way possible if they didn't reveal where their treasure was hidden. But it was no use. Again and again the travelers cried out and claimed that they had nothing at all to steal and were only poor people who had lost everything they owned when their ship, the *Gaavatanic*, had sunk.

The pirates didn't believe a word of their story and they became angrier and angrier. "Mad Moe" was the angriest pirate. He was always angry, even when there was nothing to be angry about. Now he was angrier than he had ever been before. "Put the prisoners in chains!" he shouted, as Jealous Jake turned the pirate ship around and began steering it back to the pirates' fortress, towing the small boat behind it.

"I hope they get 'The Ultimate Punishment,'" cried "Cruel Carlos," the meanest pirate of all. He knew that, according to "pirate law," they had to take the prisoners to Supreme Pirate Court before they could decide what would be done with them.

And so, once the *Anavah* boat was docked securely on the shores of the Pirates' island, the weary travelers were brought in chains into the Pirate fortress to the Supreme Pirate Court to stand trial before the Pirate Tribunal.

The frightened prisoners made their way slowly through the courtroom, dragging the heavy balls chained to their legs. They stood before the bench and trembled as they saw Crooked Kal, the Supreme Court Superior Judge, and his Bad Middos Pirate companions, Cruel Carlos and Hateful Henry, sitting there.

Then, the Chief Pirate prosecutor, Flattery Frank, cleared his throat and, in a loud voice, began to read the terrible charges against the travelers:

1. Fooling innocent pirates with an empty boat
2. Wasting the precious time of hard-working, busy pirates
3. Entering the pirates' private ocean waters without a permit
4. Lying and refusing to disclose the location of their wealth
5. Planning to rob the burger restaurant (since they had no money and were headed towards the restaurant for burgers)

The travelers weren't given any chance to speak up or defend themselves. After a long minute while the judges murmured among themselves, Cruel Carlos banged his gavel loudly on the desk. The courtroom was totally silent as Crooked Kal began to speak:

"GUILTY AS CHARGED!" he announced. Then he continued: "This court has ruled that the reason these prisoners have committed such terrible crimes is because they have the wrong middos. Therefore it has been decided that they will receive the 'Ultimate Punishment'! Let them live among us until they learn the proper way to behave! That will be the fair way to ensure that they will never commit such dishonorable deeds again! Then, when they have learned the 'correct' way to act, they will become pirates themselves and will steal enough to repay us for the treasure they failed to give us."

The prisoners were led away while all of the Pirates in the courtroom cheered.

The travelers were secretly relieved to hear what their punishment would be. It didn't sound so horrible to them compared with what they had imagined. They had been afraid that the "Ultimate Punishment" meant being thrown to the alligators, or being tortured by the pirates. But that was their first mistake. Little did they know that, in reality, their punishment would prove to be much worse.

How bad could it be to live with the Bad Middos Pirates? The passengers were convinced that it couldn't possibly hurt their middos. In fact, they were sure that their own behavior would actually have a positive influence on the pirates. Surely what they learned on Tikun Hamiddos Island had made them so strong that nothing could ever make them go back to their bad middos!

This was their second terrible mistake.

The Pirate fortress was divided into ten separate chambers. One Bad Middos Pirate, along with his own small family of pirates, inhabited each chamber.

Each of the ten pirates chose which prisoners he would like to have as his slaves, and took those prisoners to his own chamber. There the prisoners would work until their own behavior was changed to resemble that of the Pirates with whom they lived.

THE TEN BAD

- Has no concern about what others think; has no shame, and sins without guilt.
- Is argumentative, jealous, and disrespectful to people and to Hashem.
- Has no respect for anyone including his parents and those that are older and wiser than he is.
- Ridicules the Torah and those that respect it and is insensitive to basic human feelings.

CHUTZPAH DICK

HATEFUL HENRY

- Can't tolerate people or their mistakes and gets aggravated easily by things that don't go his way.
- Is quick to criticize and sees only the negative traits in other people.
- Hates people for no reason at all and doesn't appreciate the good qualities in human beings.
- Is always annoyed, bitter, and antagonistic towards others and enjoys being enraged and irritated.

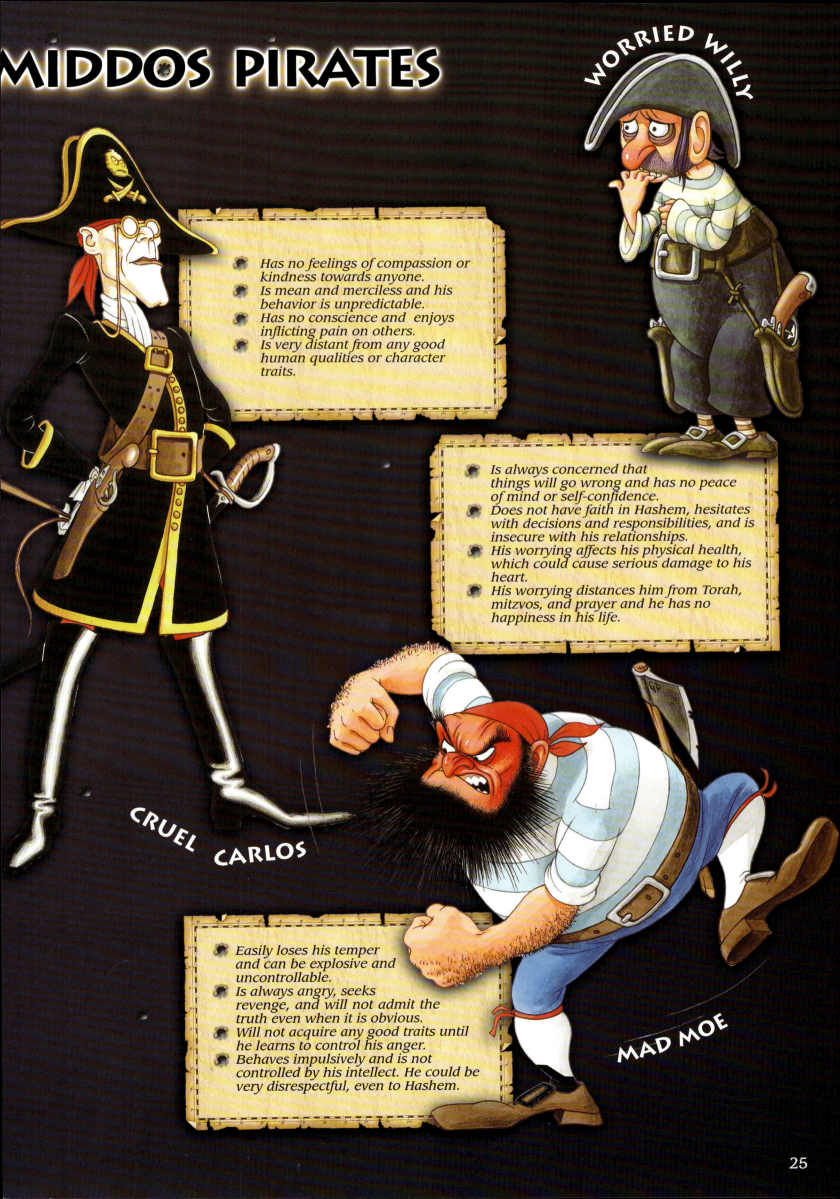

- Is extremely cheap and selfish and will not give any charity or care about the poor.
- Will never give in to compromise and has to feel that he always has the upper hand and is getting the best out of every deal.
- Will not share his belongings and will not allow others to derive any benefit from him or anything he owns without great financial compensation.
- Will not spend money on himself or on his own family's needs, not even to learn Torah or perform mitzvos.

CROOKED KAL

- Has no appreciation for the truth and will distort reality for absolutely no reason.
- Is dishonest in business and will cheat and steal without any hesitation.
- Intentionally falsifies facts as a matter of habit and creates falsehoods that eventually cause him severe embarrassment.
- Can never be trusted and is unreliable in business or as a friend.

FLATTERY FRANK

- Makes people think they are his best friends so he can get what he wants from them.
- Compliments bad people and acts kindly towards them for ulterior motives.
- Fools people with gifts and promises just so that he can get his way.
- Bribes people to do bad things for his own selfish interests and has no boundaries for his corruption.

At first, the travelers were sure they could rebuke the pirates and correct their evil ways. However, the travelers were not at all successful because they were too insulting and critical. They didn't know how to teach good middos in a positive and refined way like their Rebbe, Rebbe Lev Tov.

As a result, the opposite happened. Slowly but surely, the negative behavior of the Bad Middos Pirates began influencing the travelers.

Every night the prisoners would come together to sleep in a small room that was set aside for them in the Pirates' Fortress. At first this worked out well, but after a while the travelers began teasing and annoying each other. They were no longer kind and gentle, and they spent the nights bickering and fighting among themselves.

One night as they were getting ready for bed, they had a serious discussion, and someone pointed out how, little by little, they seemed to be losing all of the good middos they had learned on Tikun Hamiddos Island. Everyone looked at each other in surprise as they realized that he was right!

"We must do something about this, or soon we will be just like the Bad Middos Pirates," one of the passengers announced. "You're right," another traveler exclaimed. "If we don't do something right away to fight the *yetzer hara*, it will destroy us and we will have no good middos left!" The others nodded their heads in agreement. But what could they do? Finally it was decided that they must find a way to get out of the Bad Middos Fortress quickly, if they were to save themselves from the terrible influences there.

But no matter how hard they tried, not one of the travelers could think of a way to get out of the clutches of the Bad Middos Pirates. Even so, they knew that they had to do *something* to help themselves. Suddenly, one of the passengers suggested setting up an emergency *Tehillim* hour. "What a good idea," everyone agreed. "Hashem will surely help us escape from here." They decided to wait until dark when the Pirates would all be asleep and wouldn't hear them. Later on that night, when the *Tehillim* hour arrived, the travelers stood together and began reciting *Tehillim*. Their voices echoed together, and everyone felt the power of their prayers.

Then, just before the *chazan* finished, he tripped over something that was sticking out of the floor. Bending down to see what it was, he noticed some sort of handle. He pulled and tugged at it until – a section of the floor suddenly opened. He realized that he had discovered a trap door. "This must be a secret escape hatch that the Pirates prepared to use if they ever have to flee from their enemies!" he thought excitedly. Then he began to shout to the others, "Our prayers have been answered! We have a way to escape!" They all crowded around to see what he had discovered. "Let's go through this trap door quickly. I am sure that it leads to a secret way out," he advised.

But not everyone was in agreement about leaving the fortress. Some were scared that they might be caught and even killed for trying to escape. They continued to argue for several minutes, until finally they were all convinced they must do everything they could to get out of the fortress as soon as possible. They realized that staying in the fortress would destroy their middos and this would be even more dangerous for their *neshamos*. "If a person has bad middos, what is his life worth anyway?" the *chazan* pointed out. "If we have a chance to get out of here, we must take advantage of it at once!"

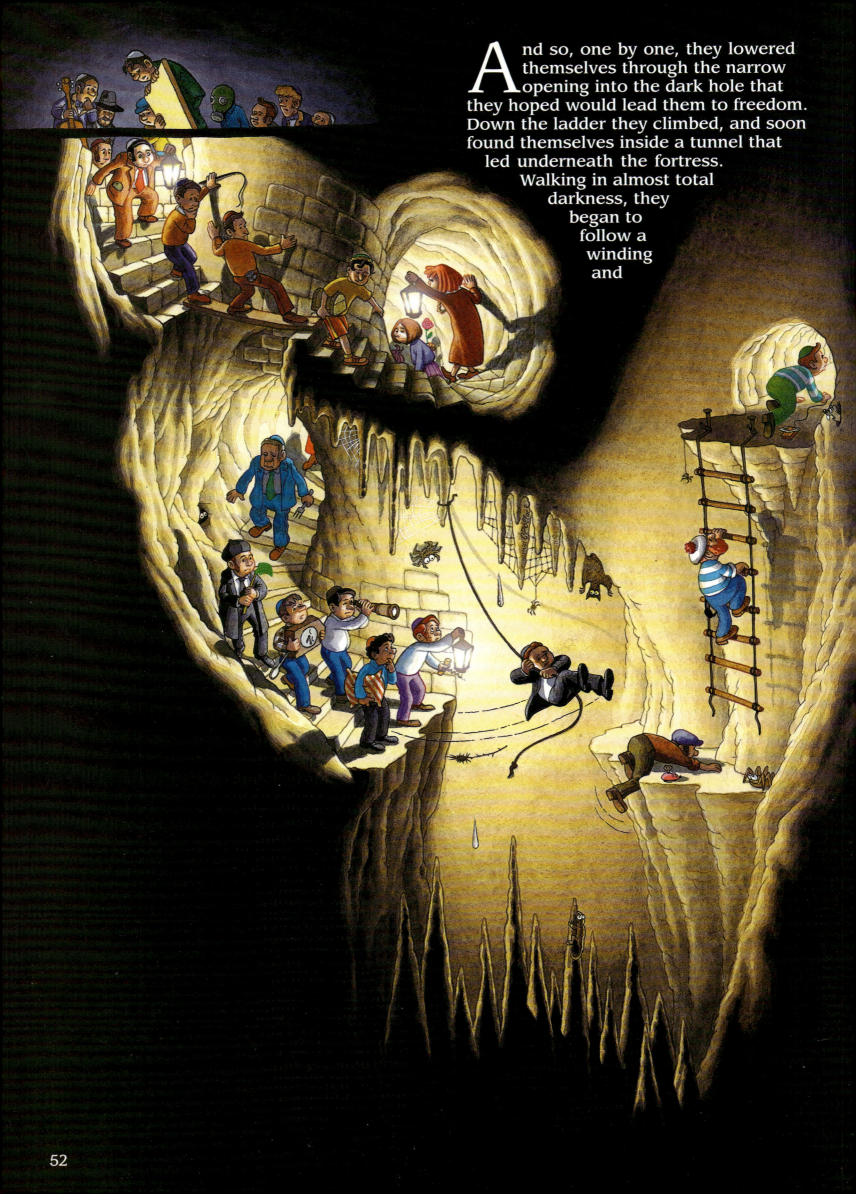

treacherous path, filled with dangers at every turn.
  When they finally saw the light at the end of the tunnel, everyone was very excited. They were sure that they had found the way to freedom. But they were in for a sad surprise. What they found was the place where their boat had been towed. But the giant gate was locked, and they could not get out. If only they had been patient and thorough, they might have found the key, but in all the tumult and excitement, nobody noticed it.

The travelers realized they were stuck in the mud at the bottom of the fortress, without the slightest idea of what to do next.

The only thing left was to go back up to the Bad Middos Pirates and face severe punishment - maybe even death - for trying to escape.

Would they just have to accept their fate and live with the frightening thought that there was no way out? Could it be that for the rest of their lives they would have to live with the unbearable Bad Middos Pirates and continue to sink lower and lower under their terrible influence?

Being under the influence of bad middos is like being stuck in quicksand. At first you don't notice that you are being affected and when you finally realize the problem it is often too late. And just like quicksand, if you are not trained to get out, the harder you struggle the deeper and deeper you sink in.

The travelers were disgusted and frustrated and began having feelings of despair and hopelessness, which is the worst tactic of the *yetzer hara*.

The *yetzer hara* is like a fly, always buzzing around our heads, trying to annoy and disturb us. He attacks us where and when we are most vulnerable and weak, and sticks to our wounds, so that we can never get rid of him.

The travelers were just about to give up when suddenly Captain Jack pointed to something outside the iron gates and began yelling.

Then suddenly, someone pointed to a small, green boat floating in the distance, and the passengers recognized this as the boat of their revered Rebbe, Rebbe Lev Tov, whom they hadn't seen for such a long time.

Everyone began waving and yelling at the boat, trying to attract Rebbe Lev Tov's attention. They were sure that he was coming to save them from the evils of the Bad Middos Pirates! Seeing Rebbe Lev Tov's boat gave them the hope and renewed strength they needed to pull themselves out of their desperate situation. They excitedly ran back up to the fortress to greet their Rebbe.

No one stopped to think about how Rebbe Lev Tov would deal with the dangerous, threatening Pirates.

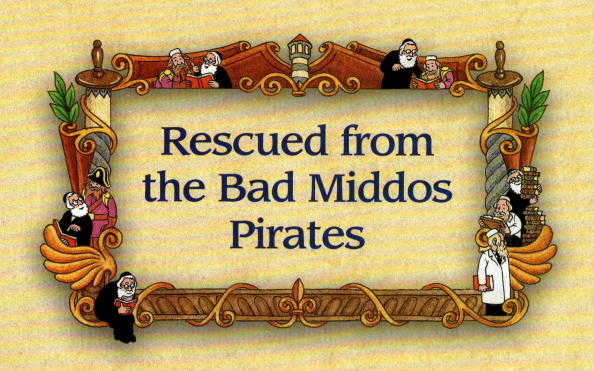

Rescued from the Bad Middos Pirates

MIDDOS SERIES 4

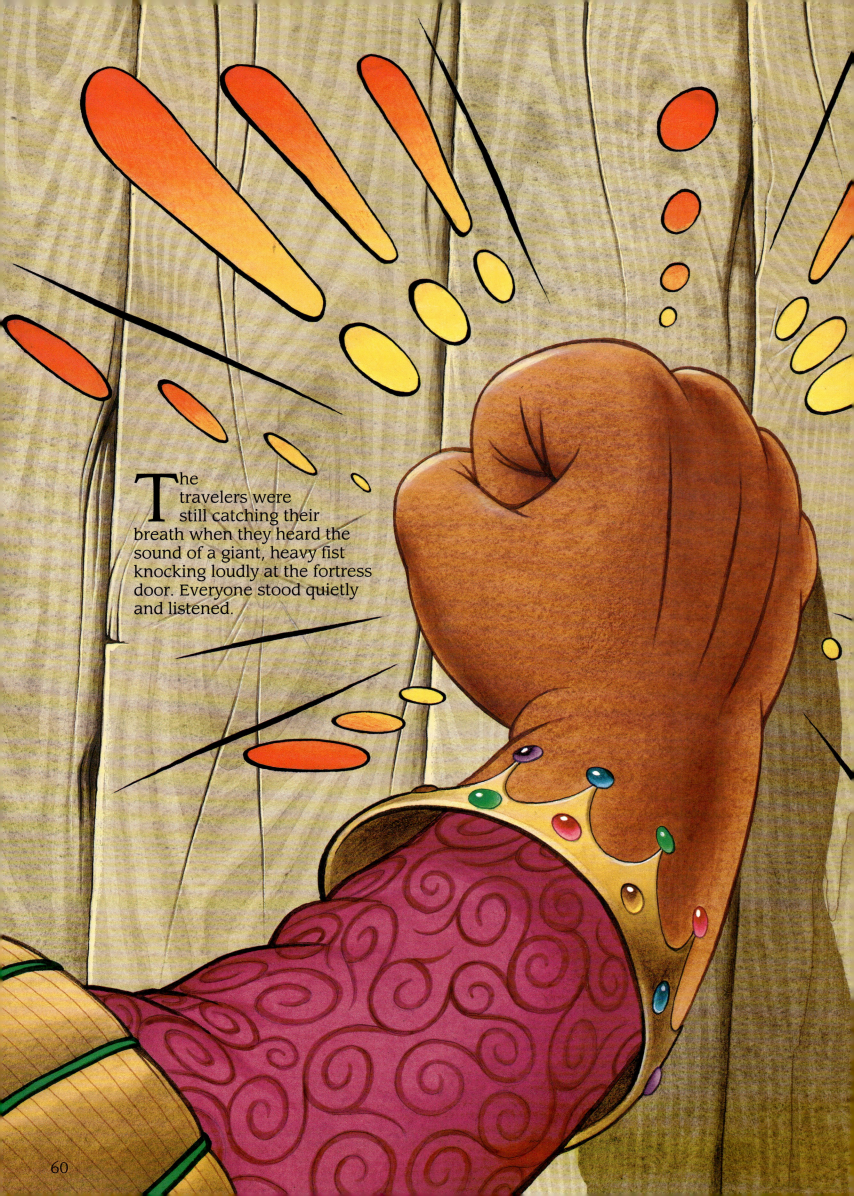

The travelers were still catching their breath when they heard the sound of a giant, heavy fist knocking loudly at the fortress door. Everyone stood quietly and listened.

At the front door, the Pirate guard, Jealous Jake, peered through the peephole and began to shout: "Attention! Attention all Pirates! Our chief has returned! Our chief has returned!" When the travelers heard this, they snuck out of their room to see what was happening, and quickly found a hiding place, from which they could stand and see everything that was unfolding below.

The huge gate swung open and every Pirate quickly fell into line where they stood silently to salute their chief, the fierce and ferocious Chief Haughty Heart, the Big Boasting Gaavah Pirate.

The passengers were absolutely stunned and confused as they watched the Pirates greet the mean Pirate who seemed far more dangerous than any of the others. "Why, this must be their leader!" whispered Captain Jack.

All of the travelers became frightened as they wondered about what they had just seen.

What was going on? Who was this scary Pirate Chief? Why was he on Rebbe Lev Tov's green boat and where was Rebbe Lev Tov? Was Rebbe Lev Tov okay, or had this mean Pirate harmed him when he stole the green boat? What would the Pirate Chief do to them when he found them living at the fortress?!

The terrified *Anavah* travelers quickly ran back to their room. They were still shaking when their door opened with a loud bang, and a Pirate came in and announced: "Attention all prisoners! The chief wants to meet with you in his chambers immediately!"
Terrified, the prisoners followed the Pirate to the Pirate Chief's private room.

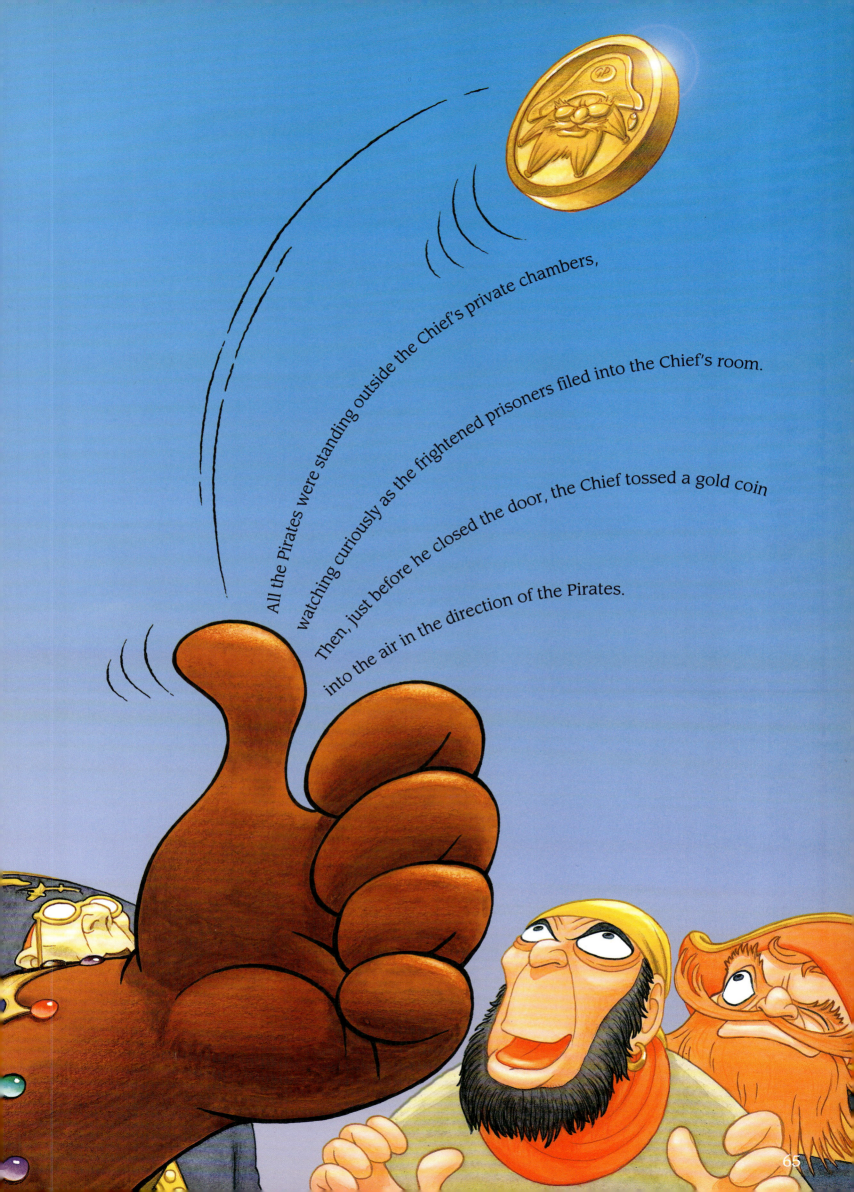

All the Pirates were standing outside the Chief's private chambers, watching curiously as the frightened prisoners filed into the Chief's room. Then, just before he closed the door, the Chief tossed a gold coin into the air in the direction of the Pirates.

The Pirates fell over each other excitedly, each one fighting to grab the coin for himself.
Then the door was tightly shut, and the chief was alone with the travelers.

FIRST HE TOOK OFF HIS GLOVES...

THEN HIS JACKET...

Once inside, the Chief turned to the trembling prisoners and began speaking in a very gentle, refined way. The prisoners listened to his words and realized that there was something very familiar about the Chief's voice. It reminded them of their beloved Rebbe Lev Tov! How could that be? Then the Chief began to explain:

"My dear friends," he said softly. "I apologize for upsetting and confusing you. Please don't be frightened by my mean and haughty appearance. Indeed, I was once very mean and haughty, but now I'm not that way at all."

As he spoke, he began to change—right before their eyes. First he took off his gloves, then his jacket, then his hat, and finally his glasses.

"Let me tell you who I really am. Sometimes it takes a person many years to understand who he really is, and who he can become. In my life, I was several different people. It took me a very long time until I realized who I could be, and who I wanted to be. Then I worked very long and hard to become that person, changing and improving myself many, many times.

THEN HIS HAT...

AND FINALLY HIS GLASSES.

"I was once the Great Pirate Chief, Haughty Heart, until one day, some years ago, when I left the Pirates, to become Rebbe Lev Tov. All of you know me as your Rebbe. You have nothing to fear from me, and I will always protect you. The Pirates still know me as their Chief, so if I had come here today dressed as Rebbe Lev Tov, they would not have recognized me and probably would have killed me.

"Let me explain to you what has happened to me, and how my life has changed.

"I have with me two maps that show exactly what my life has been like.

"**The first map** shows the route I took when I was young and foolish and did not follow any plan. I just followed the wind, without having any goal or destination. Too often, the waters were rough, and the current was too strong, and I was swept away to dangerous places without even realizing how I got there.

"**The second map** shows my good fortune in finding someone who taught me the secret of how to chart a course to a specific destination and then stick to the plan, in order to get there without mishap. Knowing how to stay on course can make a journey both meaningful and fulfilling. With this map, I learned where I should be heading and what route to take so that I could avoid any dangers I might encounter along the way."

"I dreamed that one day I could go back and teach all the Bad Middos Pirates the correct path and undo all the terrible damage that I had caused, but I knew that first I must work to improve myself.

"After you all left the island of Tikun Hamiddos, I was concerned for your safety, and so I decided to follow you to make certain that you arrived safely at your destination. You were the 100th ship that I had helped, and that was the exact number that my Rebbe had told me to help before I could follow him to Eretz Yisrael. He gave me his blessings and changed my name to Rebbe Lev Tov, the name that I use today. When I saw that you were captured by my old friends, I knew that your lives were in danger, and realized that it was finally time to help the people whom I had turned into Pirates. I must teach them everything I have learned.

"And now, my dear friends," Rebbe Lev Tov told the *Anavah* travelers, "I want to point out to you four important lessons that you can learn from your own experience.

1. Temptation can take you very far from your planned destination.
2. Even people with the best middos can be affected by negative influences.
3. Never give up in your struggle to stay on the right path because Hashem will always provide you with help in unexpected ways.
4. It is never too late to do *teshuvah*.

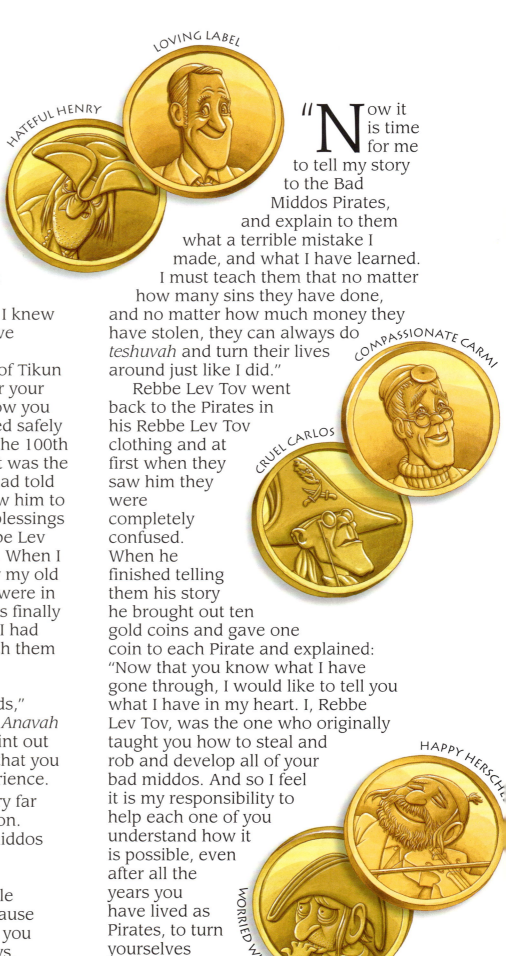

"Now it is time for me to tell my story to the Bad Middos Pirates, and explain to them what a terrible mistake I made, and what I have learned. I must teach them that no matter how many sins they have done, and no matter how much money they have stolen, they can always do *teshuvah* and turn their lives around just like I did."

Rebbe Lev Tov went back to the Pirates in his Rebbe Lev Tov clothing and at first when they saw him they were completely confused. When he finished telling them his story he brought out ten gold coins and gave one coin to each Pirate and explained: "Now that you know what I have gone through, I would like to tell you what I have in my heart. I, Rebbe Lev Tov, was the one who originally taught you how to steal and rob and develop all of your bad middos. And so I feel it is my responsibility to help each one of you understand how it is possible, even after all the years you have lived as Pirates, to turn yourselves around and

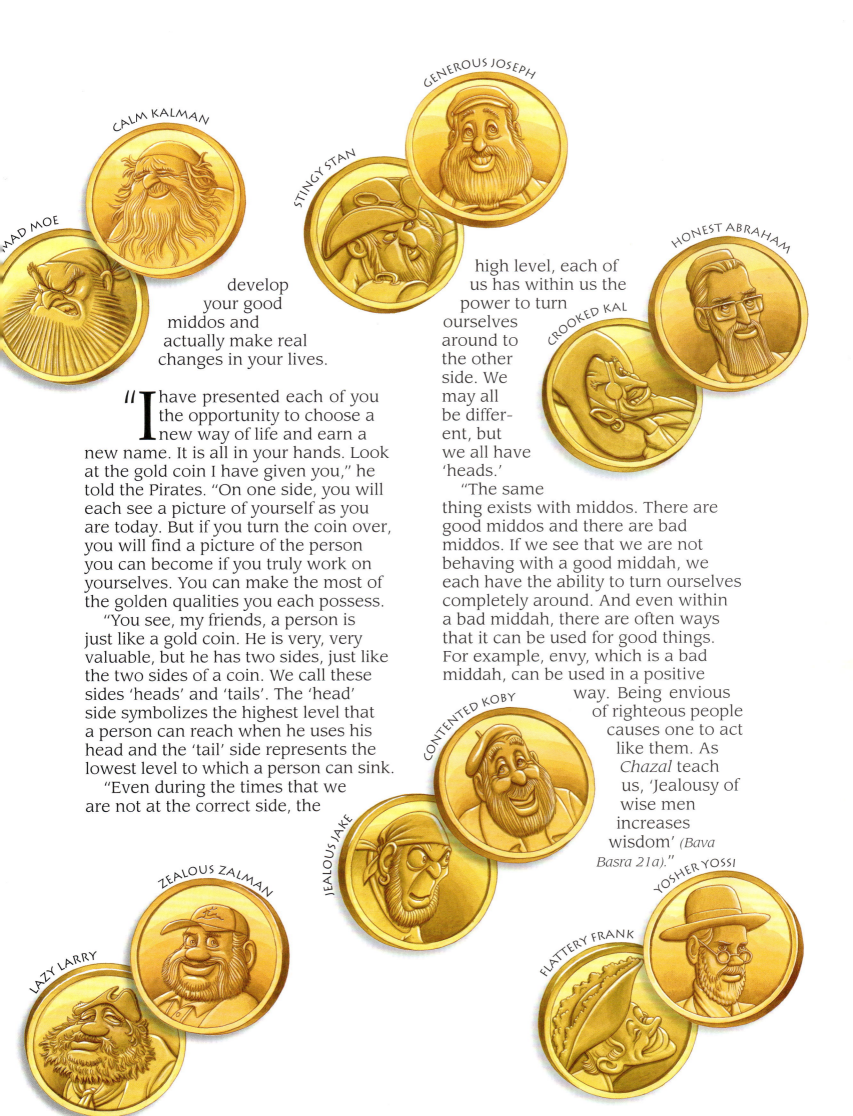

develop your good middos and actually make real changes in your lives.

"I have presented each of you the opportunity to choose a new way of life and earn a new name. It is all in your hands. Look at the gold coin I have given you," he told the Pirates. "On one side, you will each see a picture of yourself as you are today. But if you turn the coin over, you will find a picture of the person you can become if you truly work on yourselves. You can make the most of the golden qualities you each possess.

"You see, my friends, a person is just like a gold coin. He is very, very valuable, but he has two sides, just like the two sides of a coin. We call these sides 'heads' and 'tails'. The 'head' side symbolizes the highest level that a person can reach when he uses his head and the 'tail' side represents the lowest level to which a person can sink.

"Even during the times that we are not at the correct side, the high level, each of us has within us the power to turn ourselves around to the other side. We may all be different, but we all have 'heads.'

"The same thing exists with middos. There are good middos and there are bad middos. If we see that we are not behaving with a good middah, we each have the ability to turn ourselves completely around. And even within a bad middah, there are often ways that it can be used for good things. For example, envy, which is a bad middah, can be used in a positive way. Being envious of righteous people causes one to act like them. As *Chazal* teach us, 'Jealousy of wise men increases wisdom' *(Bava Basra 21a).*"

The Pirates were still in shock to hear *mussar* from the very person who had taught them to become rotten, thieving Pirates. But, listening to Rebbe Lev Tov, they realized that their life of stealing, cheating, and frightening innocent people was no way to live. If their own Chief who had everything they could dream of could make such incredible changes in his life, they understood that they could also eventually turn themselves around.

Rebbe Lev Tov taught them what the book "The Path of the Righteous" said, and explained the difference between a Bad Middah Pirate *and a Good Middah Person:*

BRAZENNESS (CHUTZPAH)

- One who is brazen has no shame; he does every evil and is not embarrassed.
- One who intensifies the trait of brazenness within himself is disliked by people even though he may be wise.
- Every sin in the Torah is unimportant to one who is brazen.
- Brazenness brings one to embarrass others and a brazen person goes to *Gehinnom* (Avos 5:20).
- A brazen person will do a great number of sins yet consider himself righteous.

CHUTZPAH DICK

RESPECT (MODESTY)

- Modesty, the quality of being respectful can only exist within someone who has intelligence.
- Through modesty and respect one will be able to attain most of the other positive traits while refraining from sin.
- A person's sense of respect and modesty towards his fellow man will prevent him from committing sins and other undesirable behavior.
- If someone commits a sin and then feels ashamed of his act, all his sins are forgiven (Berachos 12b).
- Someone who has the quality of shame and modesty will feel bad if he causes embarrassment to someone else.
- There is no level higher than that of a person who is embarrassed from doing wrong both publicly and privately because he realizes that Hashem is watching him.

RESPECTFUL REUVEN

HATRED

🔹 There is a prohibition in the Torah concerning the characteristic of Hate. *"Do not hate your brother in your heart"* (Vayikra 19:17).

🔹 The worst type of hatred is the hatred that people have for those who are righteous.

🔹 The characteristic of hatred is the cause for many sins:

- Slander
- Rejoicing at someone's misfortune
- Causing damage to others
- Taking revenge
- Not having mercy
- Always being dissatisfied and only seeing the negative aspects of others

HATEFUL HENRY

LOVE

🍃 When one utilizes love properly it is the best of traits. *"You should love Hashem your G-d"* (Devarim 6:5).

🍃 Proper love for one's children will motivate them to do whatever is needed so they will become *yirei Shamayim*.

🍃 One should love his friends and all of Israel with a total love. *"Love your friend as yourself"* (Vayikra 19:18).

🍃 If one acts with love towards everyone, when he is in need many people will come to his aid.

🍃 One develops a love for his fellow man by:

- Helping those in need
- Sharing possessions with others
- Being honest in business
- Not being petty
- Benefiting others

LOVING LABEL

CRUELTY

🏴 The trait of cruelty exists within the wicked. Cruelty is also a trait of the impudent.

🏴 A mean person has no sympathy or kindness.

🏴 A cruel person is very far from any good character traits and shows no mercy towards the poor and the suffering.

🏴 It is an act of cruelty for one to steal even a penny from his friend, thereby causing him distress.

🏴 Even when dealing with animals one must refrain from cruelty.

🏴 When anger overwhelms a person, the trait of mercy leaves him and cruelty becomes powerful within him, causing destruction and ruin.

🏴 When cruelty is in a person's soul, it brings forth a desire for revenge from his enemies.

🏴 One who causes his fellow Jew distress has transgressed a Torah commandment.

🏴 Do not reprimand someone in a cruel manner. *"Reprimand your neighbor but do not bear a sin because of him."* (Vayikra 19:17)

CRUEL CARLOS

COMPASSION

💊 Compassion is a very praiseworthy quality; it is one of the thirteen attributes of Hashem.

💊 One should try to use compassion in as many situations as possible.

💊 Punishing a child in order to teach him the path of Torah appears to be cruel. However, in truth it is the greatest kindness.

💊 One should have compassion for his relatives.

💊 One should have compassion for the poor, especially for those who fear Hashem.

💊 The characteristic of compassion is a sign that one is a descendant of Avraham Avinu.

💊 One must show mercy for animals. *"Help him lift [the animal]"* (Devarim 22:4).

💊 Great reward is given to one who speaks to the poor in a caring and merciful manner. *"One who gives a penny to the poor is blessed with six blessings, and one who consoles him [the poor person] with kind words is blessed with eleven blessings"* (Bava Basra 9b).

COMPASSIONATE CARMI

WORRY

🍃 Worry is a trait that is bad in most aspects.

🍃 Worry and sorrow cause physical illnesses that destroy the heart.

🍃 One who worries over material things is very far from Torah, mitzvos, and prayer.

🍃 All good things stem from joy and bad things stem from worry.

🍃 Great people possess no signs of worry.

🍃 A person's worrying should be limited to spiritual matters only.

🍃 One should only be worried about the sins that one has committed. *"About what should a living man be concerned? A strong man for his sins"* (Eichah 3:39).

🍃 What brings a person to complete faith in Hashem? It is not to fear any evil that happens to him, accepting everything with joy.

WORRIED WILLY

HAPPINESS

🍃 Joy comes to a person as a result of great tranquility in his heart that is unmarred by sadness. *"A joyful heart is good for the health"* (Mishlei 17:22).

🍃 An integral part of joy is accepting that everything that occurs in this world is the will of Hashem, whether it appears to be good or bad.

🍃 One who believes and trusts completely in the help of Hashem will always be happy.

🍃 One who does a mitzvah joyfully receives a reward a thousand times greater than one who does a mitzvah and feels that it is a burden.

🍃 Only when one is in a joyous mood will prophecy rest on him; therefore prophets used music for inspiration. *"And it was when the musician played and the Hand of Hashem was upon him"* (Melachim II 3:15).

HAPPY HERSCHEL

79

 ANGER

🍂 Anger is a sickness of the soul. "One who loses his temper suffers all the pains of Gehinnom" (*Nedarim* 22a).

🍂 Even the *Shechinah* is unimportant to one who loses his temper.

🍂 Anger causes one to forget his learning.

🍂 One who is angry does not act intelligently and will not admit to the truth.

🍂 In general an angry person will not acquire any good trait until he gets rid of his anger.

MAD MOE

 CALMNESS

🪨 There are three types of people that Hashem loves; one of them is a person who controls his temper (*Pesachim* 113b).

🪨 One who is calm accepts the situation that Hashem decrees for him without complaint.

🪨 One who is at ease is satisfied with his portion.

🪨 One who is at ease will forgive and pardon those who have harmed him and will act leniently towards them. The prayers of one who acts leniently towards others will surely be heard.

🪨 A calm, gracious person is willing to concede to the opinion of others.

🪨 Only the one who is wise, far seeing, and gracious without anger, is able to delve deeply into the unity and comprehension of Hashem.

CALM KALMAN

JEALOUSY

- Jealousy is a branch of anger.
- If jealousy becomes strong in a person it will lead to the desire for other people's possessions.
- One should not be jealous of a sinner's success. *"Let your heart not be envious of sinners, rather be in fear of Hashem all the day"* (Mishlei 23:17).
- Jealousy is the result of a feeling of inferiority and it leads to arguments.
- Jealousy is like a physical illness.
- Jealousy causes one to be dissatisfied with himself.
- One should act in a manner that will not cause others to be jealous of him. *"Do not put a stumbling block in front of a blind man"* (Vayikra 19:14).

JEALOUS JAKE

CONTENTMENT

- Who is wealthy? One who is content with his portion (*Avos 4:1*).
- One should be content with what one has. A person should not be argumentative, envious, or lustful nor should he pursue honor (*Sefer Chasidim chap. 51*).
- Hashem resides among the Jewish people only when they are unified with "one heart," without jealousy, similar to the ministering angels… (*Sefer Chareidim chap. 74*).
- If one loses his money he should not worry nor mourn his loss; rather, he should thank G-d as he did when G-d gave the money to him. He should be content with his lot and not seek anyone's misfortune, nor should he desire anyone's money… (*Chovos Halevavos – Preface Shaar HaBitachon*).
- One should realize that what others have is not available at all to him. In this way he will be content and saved from envy; he will not desire what belongs to others. He should be satisfied with whatever Hashem has allotted to him. (*Derashos of the Maharal – Derashah of Shabbos Shuvah*).

CONTENTED KOBY

LAZINESS

- The affairs of a person who is overcome by the trait of laziness are ruined in this world and in the next.

- A lazy person likes leisure and therefore he will not exert the effort to grow in Torah and mitzvos. Even when he sits in the synagogue, he sleeps.

- Because a lazy person does not put out effort he is not fit for this world or for the World to Come.

- The lazy person is far removed from good traits.

- Because a lazy person does not exert himself to learn Torah correctly, his reasoning will be incorrect.

- 'One who is too lazy to articulate words of Torah', there is no laziness greater than this.

LAZY LARRY

ZELOUSNESS

- Zealousness is an important trait for accomplishment in Torah and mitzvos.

- Zealousness is a trait that the righteous employ in their service to Hashem.

- One who does good deeds with zealousness expresses his love towards Hashem.

- Zealousness is the foundation of all good middos.

- Just as one should be zealous in things pertaining to Torah and mitzvos one should be eager in all appropriate worldly matters.

ZEALOUS ZALMAN

STINGINESS

- A stingy person will not give charity and has no mercy on the poor.
- A miser will not concede anything in his dealings with other people and no one will derive any benefit from him.
- A miser has no trust in Hashem and people do not like a miser.
- A miser is not willing to expend money or energy in doing a mitzvah.
- A miser is not willing to spend any money in order to learn Torah. Therefore he will remain empty of Torah and mitzvos.

STINGY STAN

GENEROSITY

- Generosity is the trait through which a person can attain great heights both in this world and in the next.
- There are three types of generosity:
  - Generosity with one's money
  - Generosity with one's body
  - Generosity with one's wisdom
- The generosity of charity to G-d-fearing people is a hidden treasure that will never be lost and a generous person will be helped when he is in need. *"He who is kind to the poor [by giving charity] is like he is lending to Hashem"* (Mishlei 19:17).
- The perfectly generous man is the one who always gives, no matter whether it is a large or small amount, even before he is asked.
- The trait of generosity is like lending to Hashem. Charity is great because it accompanies those who practice it when they depart this world.
- One should be generous with his Torah knowledge, teaching others and bringing them closer to Hashem. This is the greatest form of generosity.

GENEROUS JOSEPH

DISHONESTY

🥔 Lying is like worshiping idols. *"One who changes his words is like one who serves idols"* (Sanhedrin 92a).

🥔 One who tells a small lie will eventually bear false witness. *"One who speaks falsehoods will be a false witness."* (Mishlei 6:19).

🥔 One who wishes to be an honest man must work to rid himself of all negative traits so that he will be able to attain the truth.

🥔 The punishment of a liar is great; even when he tells the truth he is not believed. *"Falsehood has no feet"* [it does not stand long because it will eventually be discovered as being false] (Sanhedrin 89b).

🥔 One should not lie in business matters nor cause anyone to lie because of him and one should stay away from people who lie.

🥔 It takes great wisdom to avoid telling a falsehood because the *yetzer hara* always lies in wait to entrap a person.

🥔 It is prohibited to tell a story and change some of the facts even though this does not result in loss to anyone. *"It is forbidden to deceive people, even non-Jews. This is a sin; we are obligated to speak the truth because this is one of the foundations of the soul"* (Chulin 94a).

CROOKED KAL

HONESTY

The soul is created in Heaven and is carved out from the throne of Hashem. In Heaven there is no falsehood, only truth. *"And Hashem Elokim is true"* (Yirmiyahu 10:10).

Hashem, Who is the personification of Truth, draws near to those who call to Him in truth. *"Hashem is near to those who call to Him in truth"* (Tehillim 145:18).

Truth must be in a person's heart, not only on his lips. One who speaks only the truth will live a long life.

There is no quality like someone who speaks the truth. *"The beginning of your word is truth"* (Tehillim 119:160). *"Keep away from a false thing"* (Shemos 23:7).

One should not lie to a Jew or to a non-Jew and should not even hint to an untruth. *"The remnant of Israel should not commit an injustice and should not speak untruth and there should not be found in their mouth deceit"* (Tzefaniah 3:13).

When there is truth in the world Hashem looks down upon the earth with justice. *"Truth grows out of the earth and justice will look down from heaven"* (Tehillim 85:12).

HONEST ABRAHAM

FLATTERY

👄 Rabbi Elazar said, "Everyone who has flattery within him brings anger upon the world" *(Sotah 41b)*.

👄 Flattery includes the following:

- Someone who recognizes that his friend is wicked and a liar but flatters him and says he has done nothing wrong. *"Those that abandon the Torah will praise wicked people" (Mishlei 28:4)*. *"One who justifies the wicked and condemns the righteous, both of these are the loathing of Hashem" (Mishlei 17:15)*.

- Someone trusted by the community who appoints a relative to a position of importance, saying that he is capable, when in truth he is not. *"Whoever appoints an unqualified judge, it is as if he planted a tree for idol worship" (Sanhedrin 7b)*.

👄 One of the worst types of flatterers is one who flatters his friend to gain his confidence and then takes advantage of his trust and cheats him. *"The net is spread for no purpose in the eyes of the birds and they lie in wait for their blood and hide to capture them" (Mishlei 1:17-18)*.

👄 It is prohibited to flatter, misrepresent your intentions, or fool any person, even a non-Jew. *"The prayers of a flatterer will not be heard and he will be cursed and go to Gehinnom"*.

FLATTERY FRANK

INTEGRITY

🎩 Integrity is a character trait that is the opposite of the middah of flattery *(Nesivos Olam II, Nesiv Hatochachah, Chap. 1)*.

🎩 One who has integrity will not falsify his words or misrepresent his intentions for ulterior motives *(Maharal, Chidushei Aggados II, Sotah 79)*.

🎩 One who has the courage to stand up for his principles is a man with integrity and deserves to be blessed *(Nesivos Olam II, Nesiv Hatochachah, Chap. 1)*.

🎩 A person with integrity will have the strength of character not to be threatened by influential people and will rebuke them when appropriate *(Nesivos Olam II, Nesiv Hatochachah, Chap. 1)*.

🎩 A man with integrity will not be lured by honor and excessive pleasure, which are the major factors that bring a person to flattery.

🎩 One who seeks a life of truth and integrity will follow a path that is totally opposite the path of falsehood and flattery. *(Maharal, Chidushei Aggados II, Sotah 79)*.

YOSHER YOSSI

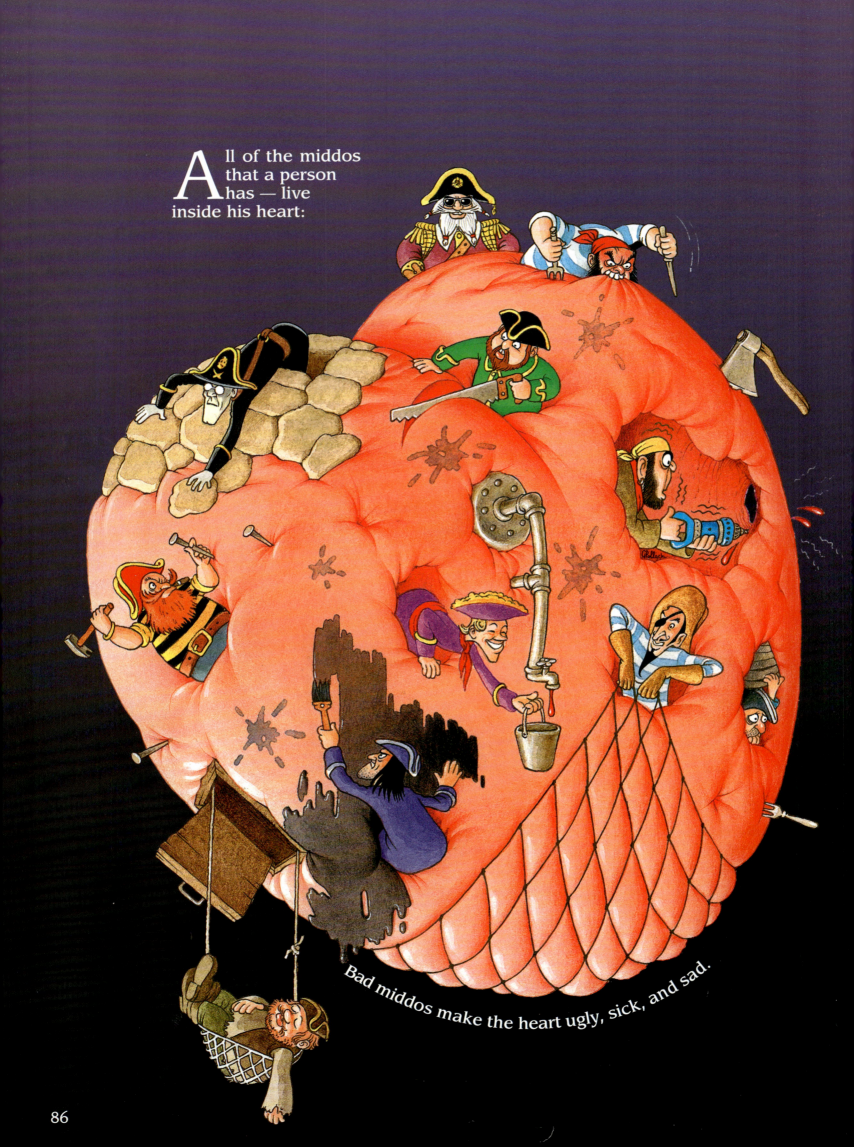

"Now," said Yankele, who was telling the story, "it's time for all of you to get up and come upstairs with me. You see, this very building in which we are standing today is the same fortress that was once used by the Pirates as the Bad Middos Fortress.

After Rebbe Lev Tov taught the Pirates how to change their ways and use their good middos, they decided to change the entire Bad Middos Fortress into a Good Middos Palace, where people from all over the world would come to learn good middos. Everyone in the Good Middos Palace was a specialist in a certain good middah and helped others develop that middah.

But you don't have to be a specialist to teach good middos. You too can teach good middos by being an example to everyone you meet. You can be a model of a Torah personality by portraying behavior that others will want to emulate. That is a true *Kiddush Hashem*.

*J*oin us in the next volume: "The Dilemmas in the Palace of Good Middos". We will analyze conflicts concerning middos, and explain how to resolve them. See you soon at the Palace!

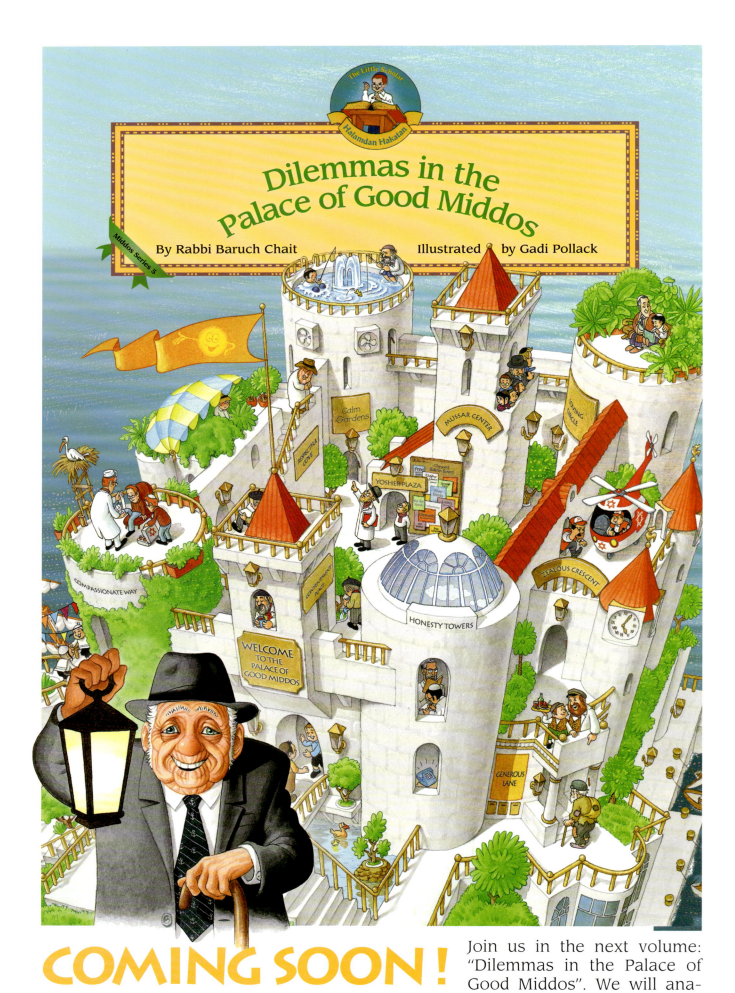

COMING SOON!

Join us in the next volume: "Dilemmas in the Palace of Good Middos". We will analyze conflicts concerning middos, and explain how to resolve them. See you soon at the Palace!

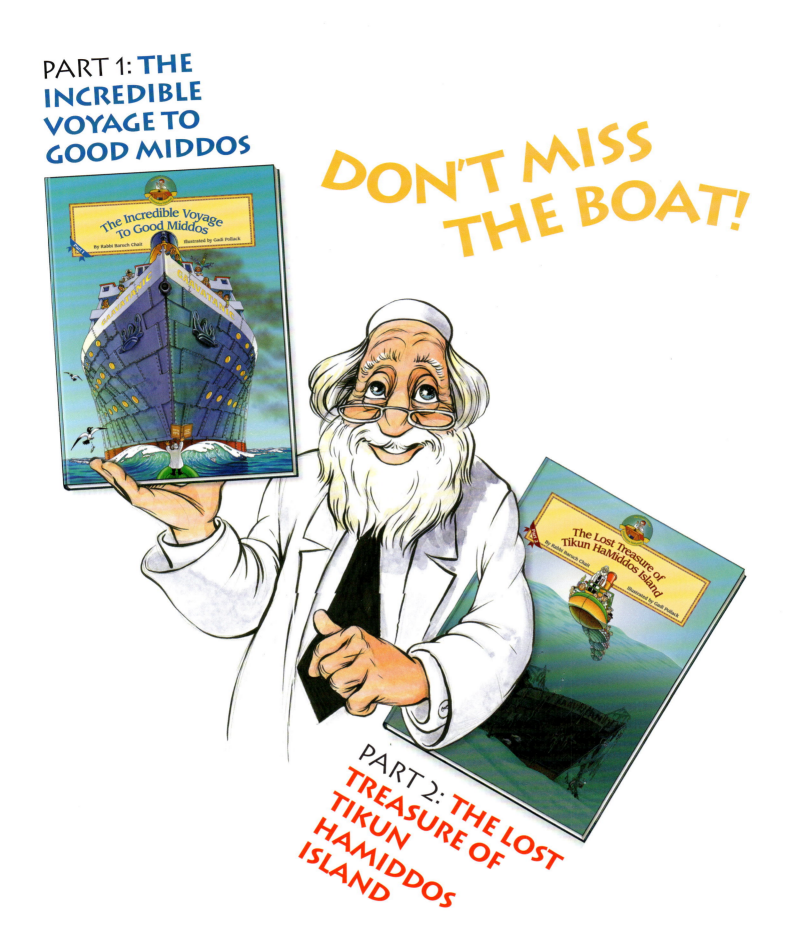

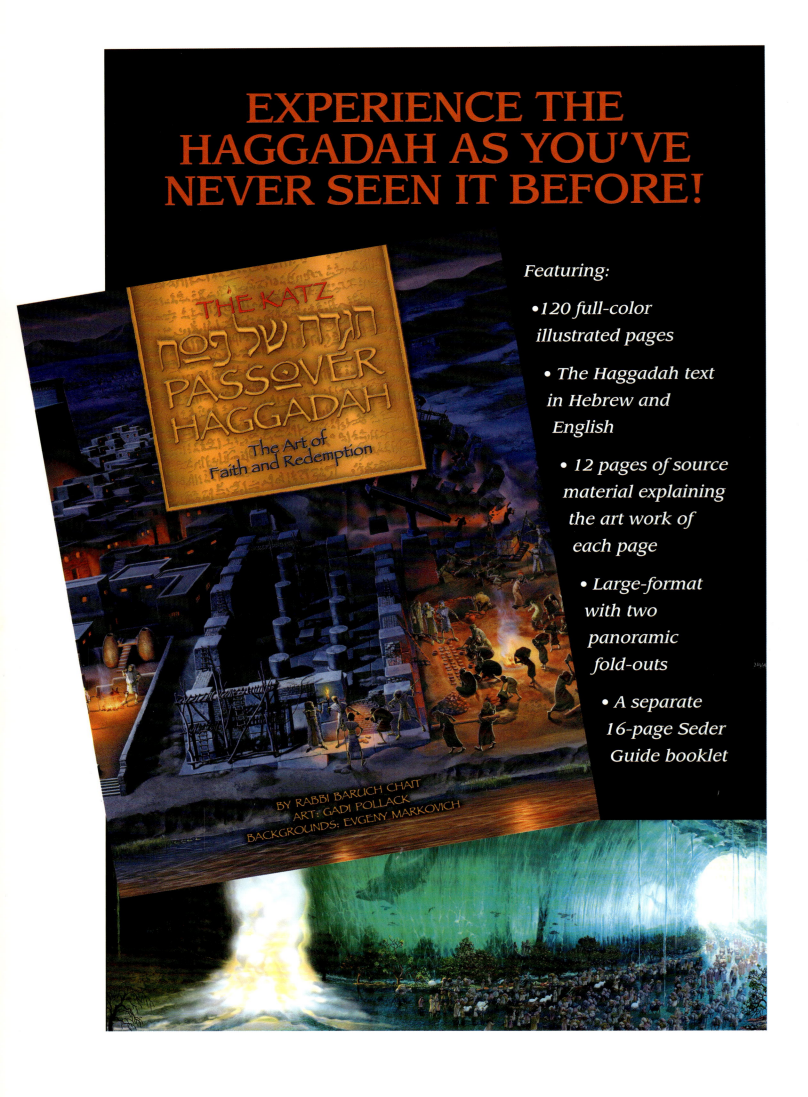

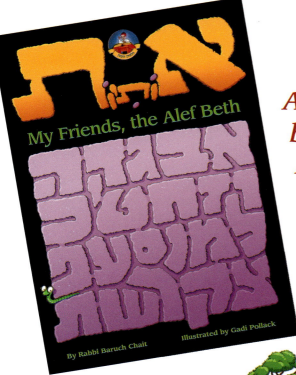

Another bestseller by Halamdan Hakatan, about to hit the market!

✹ *Search for object starting with each Hebrew letter!*

✹ *Learn many new words in Hebrew!*

✹ *Learn the numerical equivalent of each letter!*

✹ *Recognize different forms of each letter: hand written, Torah letters, and Rashi script.*

✹ *It's a great gift and a fantastic learning device. Have loads of fun with your kids as they get to know each of these charming and indispensable characters.*

An educational experience with incredibly exciting artwork, every parent and grandparent would want their children and grandchildren to have this remarkable book. Brilliantly animated, the hebrew letters come alive and will become you children's dearest friends.

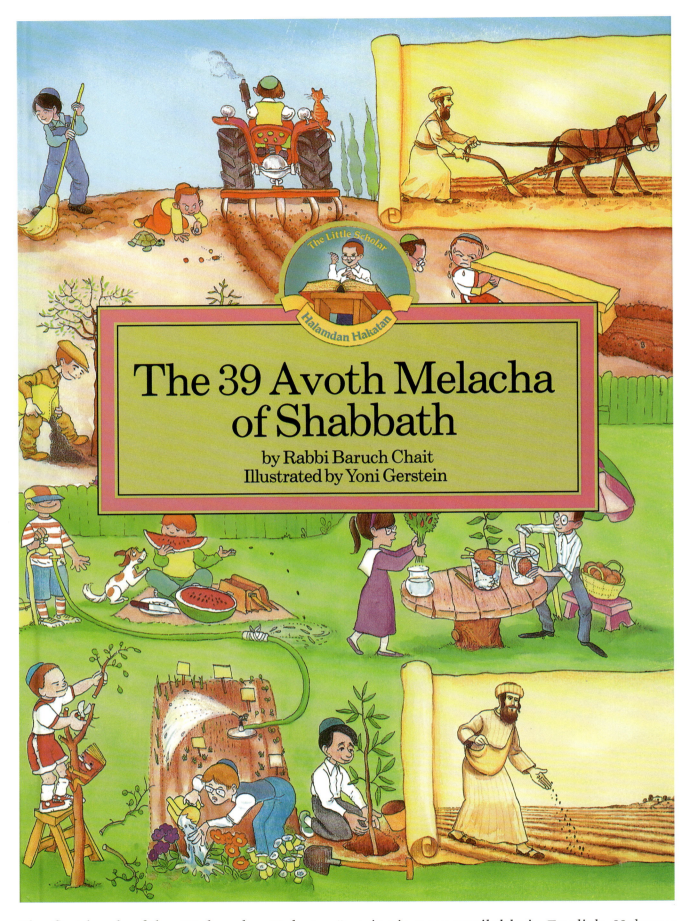

The first book of the "Halamdan Hakatan" series is now available in English, Hebrew, French, Yiddish and Spanish. Everyone should have this wonderful "best selling" book in their home. Excellent for children and adults.